MW00980770

Lily's Walnut Tree Search

by Grace L. Darney

To Ben & Evie !

G. L
Darney
2024

Lily's Walnut Tree Search
Copyright © 2024 by Grace L. Darney

All rights reserved. No part of this publication may be reproduced, distributed, or transmitted in any form or by any means, including photocopying, recording, or other electronic or mechanical methods, without the prior written permission of the author, except in the case of brief quotations embodied in critical reviews and certain other non-commercial uses permitted by copyright law.

Tellwell Talent
www.tellwell.ca

ISBN
978-1-77941-658-2 (Hardcover)
978-1-77941-657-5 (Paperback)

In loving memory of Stewart Hyslop,
whose enthusiastic searches
for walnut trees inspired this book.

Lily swallowed her last tiny pancake, and then she asked, "Grandpa, which tree in your yard is a walnut tree?"

"We don't have one in our yard, Lily. Our yard is too small for a tree growing as tall and wide as a walnut tree. Why did you think one of my trees could be a walnut?"

Grandpa poured more maple syrup onto his pancakes as he looked at Lily.

"I just thought our town of Walnut Grove might be named after walnut trees," Lily reached for the last piece of bacon.

"Oh, aren't you the funny girl!" Grandpa laughed.

As Grandpa took his dishes to the sink, Lily asked Grandma, "Grandma, do you know if there are walnut trees nearby?"

Grandma replied, "Over a century ago, my grandparents owned an acre of walnut trees just up the hill from here that they called a walnut grove. But the land was sold and houses were built. You and Grandpa should go for a walk to see if any trees are left."

Grandpa helped Lily carry her plate to the sink. After she washed her sticky fingers, they went outside.

"You two have fun," called Grandma, closing the screen door behind them.

Grandpa held Lily's hand as they started their walk.

"It's sure warm for a mid-June day; we don't even need jackets," said Grandpa.

Lily noticed a tree next door with red fruit hanging from its branches, and she asked, "Grandpa, what is that tree?"

"It's a cherry tree, Lily. Most of those cherries are almost ready to pick."

"Yummy, can I pick some? I love cherries. Grandma makes yummy cherry pies." Lily did a little dance as they looked at the tree.

"Grandma makes the BEST cherry pies!" responded Grandpa. "Cherries are ready to eat in late June in our part of British Columbia, so maybe you can pick some two weeks from now."

"I know that tree over there. It's a maple!" cried Lily, pointing to a tree on the boulevard.

"We have a red maple leaf on our Canada flag," Grandpa said.

"I look at the maple leaf on our flag when we sing 'O Canada' at school. And, when maple leaves fall to the ground in autumn, Daddy rakes them into piles that I jump onto."

Lily jumped up and down, pretending to be jumping on piles of leaves.

"That's lots of fun, Lily. I did that when I was young, too." Grandpa then pointed to a park and said, "Let's see if there's a walnut tree over there."

Lily and Grandpa walked into the park. They saw an adventure playground ringed with tall green trees.

"Grandpa, are those tall trees walnut trees?" asked Lily.

"No, sweetie, they're red cedars. They are evergreen trees. Evergreens don't lose their leaves in the autumn like maple trees do," said Grandpa.

"Daddy called our Christmas tree a fir tree. Is that an evergreen?" asked Lily.

"Yes, they are evergreens, unless they're plastic," Grandpa smiled as he answered.

Lily laughed, and then she asked, "Why don't evergreens lose their leaves?"

"Well, Lily, their leaves are actually called needles. The needles stay green all year because they have to make food for the tree, even through winter, so that's why they are called evergreens. Trees and other plants use sunlight to make food. It's called photosynthesis. I know you learned about that in school last year."

Lily nodded, and then she joked, "I think they should be called Forever Greens."

Grandpa and Lily walked closer to the cedars.

Lily touched one, and she said, "Oooh, feel the bark, Grandpa. It's flaky. Uh oh, I pulled some off!"

"That's okay, Lily, that's how you know it's a red cedar," said Grandpa. "No other evergreen has bark like this. The cedar is sacred to First Nations people of western Canada. Long ago, they used the bark for clothes and dishes, and they used the wood to build canoes and houses and to make masks. The red cedar is still an important tree for all people."

"I love this bark," said Lily. Then she yelled, "Look, look, across the street—maybe that's a walnut tree. It sure has pretty white flowers." She carefully rolled up the piece of cedar bark and put it in her pocket as they crossed the street.

"It's an apple tree, Lily. Those are beautiful blossoms, aren't they?" Grandpa pulled a blossom from the tree and gave it to Lily. "Hold this to your nose—I call it the smell of spring."

Lily sniffed the blossom and asked, "Why are there no apples?"

"Well, it's only the middle of June, Lily. It will be a few more months before we see apples. Bees visit the blossoms to gather pollen, and then apples start to grow."

"I LOVE apple pie!" Lily skipped beside Grandpa.

"Grandma is baking an apple pie today, Lily. It will be ready for our lunch," said Grandpa.

"Goody! I bet I can eat two slices. How many can you eat?" asked Lily.

"I could eat two pies." Grandpa rubbed his tummy and smacked his lips.

"You could?" Lily thought Grandpa was serious until he winked.

"I wish we could find a walnut tree, Grandpa. Why is Walnut Grove called Walnut Grove if there are no walnut trees?" Lily was very puzzled.

"That's a real mystery, Lily-girl. Perhaps the name was kept after houses were built, even if there aren't any walnut trees left."

"I like eating walnuts. Do you like walnuts, Grandpa?"

"Yes, I like walnuts, Lily. Squirrels and other animals, and even birds, eat walnuts, too. I especially like walnuts in your Grandma's banana loaf."

Grandpa pointed to a building nearby, and he asked, "Should we stop at that ice cream shop for a wee break?"

"YES!"

They walked into the shop and checked the different flavours.

Lily wriggled close to the display. "May I have a strawberry cone, Grandpa?"

"You sure can. Your old Gramps will have maple walnut."

Lily laughed and said, "Maples and walnuts in ice cream? That's weird!"

"Well, dear, remember the maple syrup on your pancakes this morning?"

"Yes, Grandma made me tiny pancakes. I poured lots of syrup on them."

"Lily, maple syrup comes from maple trees."

"You mean the maple tree we saw near your house has syrup in it?"

"No, Lily, maple syrup comes from maple trees that grow in eastern Canada where it's much colder than here."

"How is it made?" Lily asked.

"Well, first, a small hole is made in the tree, then a hollow tube is placed in the hole. In early spring, as temperatures warm, sap rises up the tree and it dribbles out the tube into a bucket. Then the sap is boiled until it gets thicker and becomes syrup."

"Maple syrup is sap from trees? I never knew that!"

"Yes, isn't it wonderful that something so delicious comes from a tree?"

Grandpa handed Lily her cone, and he said, "Maple syrup is mixed with pieces of walnuts when the ice cream is made. It's my favourite."

"My favourite is strawberry," said Lily.

Lily licked her ice cream cone while Grandpa waited for his.

When it was ready, he asked, "Would you like a taste, Lily?"

"Yes, please!" Grandpa held out his cone. Lily bit off the pointy top. "Yum, that's delicious! When I'm grown up, maple walnut will be my favourite too."

Lily didn't offer her grandpa any of her ice cream, but he didn't mind.

"Should we find a place to sit in the shade?" asked Grandpa when they crossed the street.

"I'm going to sit under one of these shady trees we haven't seen before," said Lily.

"Lily, that's a walnut tree you're sitting under!" yelled Grandpa. "There are three walnut trees here. This area must be part of that old orchard your grandma mentioned."

"These are walnut trees? YAY! We found them," yelled Lily, so excited she bounced up and down and bumped her cone against her chin.

Grandpa wiped Lily's face with a napkin. They finished their cones and stood up to look closely at the trees.

"Lily, can you feel the deep furrows and rounded ridges of the bark? It's different from soft cedar bark," said Grandpa as they went close to the trunk of one of the walnut trees.

Lily rubbed her hands on the trunk and said, "Wow, walnut bark is very rough."

"Smell this leaf." Grandpa crushed a leaf in his fingers and held it under Lily's nose.

"I never knew leaves can have smells. This one reminds me of Christmas time and hot apple cider," she said as she smelled the leaf.

"Yes, it smells a little like cloves, which is the spice in that drink," said Grandpa.

Then Grandpa added, "Look way up. Do you see a lot of tiny round green things hanging up there? They are walnuts just beginning to grow."

"Wow, Grandpa, can we come back to pick them when they're ready?" asked Lily.

"The nuts will be too high to pick, but in September and October, ripe nuts fall to the ground, and they will be easy to gather into a bucket," answered Grandpa.

Lily chuckled and said, "I hope we get the walnuts before the squirrels crack them all open!"

"The raccoons and birds will be after them too! Now, let's head home," said Grandpa, taking Lily's sticky hand in his.

"I can't wait to tell Grandma! She'll be so happy we found walnut trees," said Lily, smiling up at her grandpa. "Hey, this is a different street from the one we walked on before. Maybe we'll find more walnut trees."

"There are lots of other trees on this street that we can look at, too. Here's a beautiful weeping willow," said Grandpa.

"Why is it called a weeping willow?" asked Lily. "Is it because the branches are so long and thin that they touch the ground and look like they're crying?"

"I'm not sure, but that could be why. I'll look in one of my tree books for the answer," replied Grandpa.

"Is this tree where Grandma gets pussy willows from?"

"No, those are from the pussy willow plant; it's a small shrub, not a tree. The pussy willow flower is called a catkin. Did you know that?"

"No, I didn't. Do they make pollen for bees like apple blossoms do?"

"Yes, Lily, they do. Bees visit pussy willows after winter is over because these are the very first plants to blossom, and bees are very hungry then. The pollen from the yellow catkins is their food. Grey tufts on the pussy willow branches that look like a cat's paw appear before the pollen."

"Is that where the plant gets its name? Because the grey fluff looks like a furry cat paw?"

"Yes, you are correct," replied Grandpa.

"I'm going to tell Grandma not to pick pussy willows too early."

"Grandma picks them when they're the grey fluff, not when the yellow pollen appears."

"She's picking little kitty paws!" Lily grinned.

Grandpa and Lily turned the corner beside the willow tree. The street was like a forest with more trees than houses. Grandpa pointed to a very tall evergreen. "This is a western hemlock," said Grandpa. "Hemlocks are so tall their tops droop over."

"Is that how you know it's a hemlock? I can't see the top of the tree, so how will I know what it is?" Lily drooped over like a tall hemlock and shouted, "I'm a hemlock, Grandpa!"

"Silly girl! I can't see the top either, Lily. But I can identify it by its needles, bark, and cones, which are different from all other evergreens."

Grandpa reached up and pulled a branch toward Lily, who exclaimed, "Gosh, Grandpa, these needles are flat and they're soft and shiny too. And look, they're yellowy-green on top but on the bottom, they're a white colour. That's neat!"

"Yes, those needles also feel a bit feathery, don't they? Look at the cones along the branch. They are very small, only about two centimetres long."

As they walked, Grandpa said, "Years ago, First Nations people used hemlock wood for many things, like spoons, combs, and serving bowls. Now it is used to build stairways, and doors, and ladders."

"I'm sure learning lots of things about trees, Grandpa," said Lily as they arrived back home.

Grandpa closed the gate and showed Lily a tree next to the front door.

"Lily, I planted this tree when your grandmother and I built our house fifty years ago. It's a dogwood tree."

"There sure are funny names in nature, Grandpa. WEEPING willows! CATkins! DOGwoods!"

"You're a very observant girl, Lily. I once heard that the dogwood tree got its name because when the branches rub together in a wind, they make a sound like a dog barking, but I've never heard that sound myself."

"If it's windy the next time I visit you, I'll listen for your tree to bark!" said Lily.

Grandpa grabbed two low branches and rubbed them together.

"Your tree isn't barking, Grandpa!" said Lily. They giggled as he opened the front door.

"The white flower of the dogwood tree is the provincial flower of British Columbia, which means you can't pick the blossoms nor cut down the tree," said Grandpa.

"I like their pretty blossoms just where they are—on the tree," said Lily, rescuing her piece of cedar bark from her pocket.

Lily yelled for Grandma, "We found three walnut trees near the ice cream shop! We sat under one to eat our ice cream cones. And we saw some tiny green walnuts starting to grow."

Grandma hugged Lily and said, "Those trees must be over one hundred years old. It's amazing that they are still growing. In the autumn, you and Grandpa can gather the ripe walnuts. I will bake them in my banana loaves."

Grandma placed bowls of creamy broccoli soup on the table, and she said, "Eat some trees, Lily."

"Grandma, what do you mean? I'm not eating a tree; I'm eating broccoli soup!"

Lily laughed when Grandma said, "Lily, pieces of broccoli look just like tiny trees."

"After we finish our tree soup, can we have apple pie?" asked Grandpa.

Grandma just shook her head when Lily said, "Grandpa can eat two pies."

While they ate their lunch, Lily told Grandma about all the trees they'd seen and how Grandpa identified each tree by looking at its bark and leaves or needles.

"Grandma, here's a piece of cedar bark that I accidentally pulled off the trunk."

"My goodness, it's very soft and stringy, Lily."

"Yes, Grandma, and that's why First Nations people used it to make clothing a long, long time ago. Maybe I can make it into a coat for my doll."

Lily asked for another piece of apple pie, and then she said, "Grandpa, next time I visit, we'll have to go for a walk to find more trees. Maybe fruit trees."

"Another tree walk is a good idea. Perhaps we can stop for an ice cream again." Grandpa winked.

"I'll go with you if we can go where my favourite tree grows," said Grandma.

"You have a favourite tree, Grandma?"

"Yes, it's the beautiful arbutus," replied Grandma. "Arbutus trees grow on rocky slopes near the ocean. They have reddish-brown bark that flakes off in long strips in the summer with smooth new bark underneath that's a light green colour."

"You mean it peels off like cedar bark? Grandpa said that the red cedar is the only tree with bark that peels."

"No, it's not the same. Arbutus bark always peels off by itself, but red cedar bark doesn't. First Nations people peeled cedar bark for special uses like making baskets or mats. They didn't take all the bark from a tree, because that would have killed it."

Grandpa interrupted, "The arbutus is Canada's only broad-leafed evergreen tree."

"What does that mean, Grandpa?" asked Lily.

"Lily, do you remember talking about how evergreens keep their needles all year long? The arbutus doesn't lose all its leaves every autumn. It doesn't have needles like evergreen trees. It has round, shiny leaves, but they don't fall off until after the new leaves grow. So, it has leaves all year, and that's why it's called an evergreen," explained Grandpa.

"I'm calling the arbutus an everLEAF tree instead of an everGREEN tree," replied Lily.

Grandma agreed that that would be a perfect name for her favourite tree, and then she said, "Soon, wild huckleberries and blueberries will be ripe, and later, blackberries for my famous blackberry and apple pie."

Lily, hugging her grandparents, said, "I can hardly wait to stay overnight again. I loved learning about trees, and next time, I'll bring lots of buckets for all the berries we'll pick!"

Printed in the USA
CPSIA information can be obtained
at www.ICGtesting.com
JSHW041236050524
62512JS00001B/1